D1372400

# FX FACES

## by SNAZAROO

Kingfisher
NEW YORK

# Contents

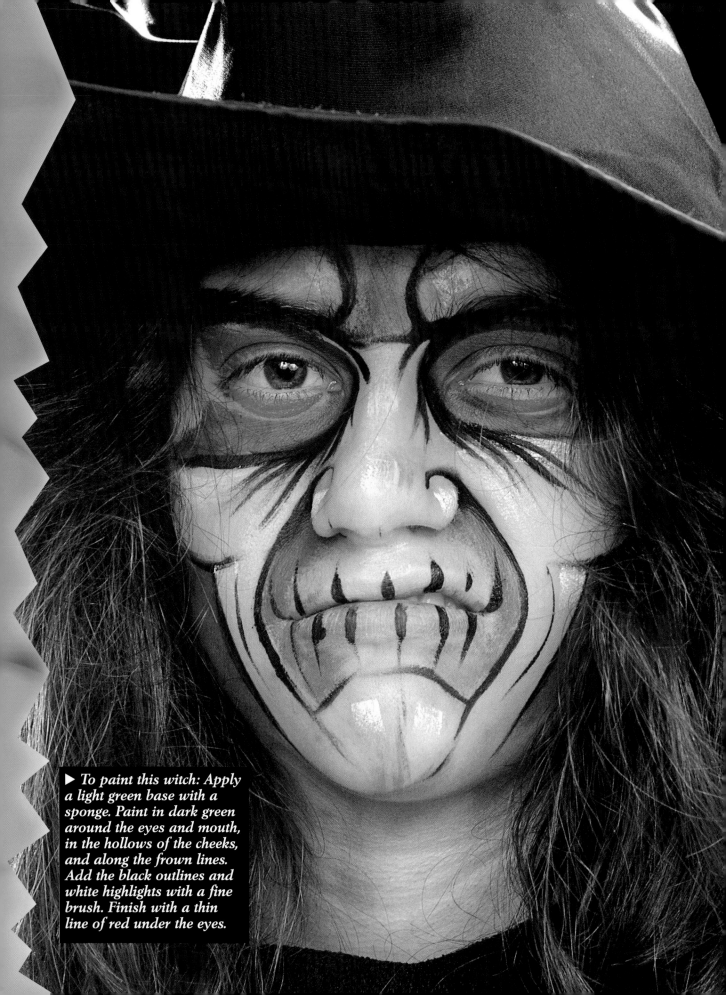

▶ *To paint this witch: Apply a light green base with a sponge. Paint in dark green around the eyes and mouth, in the hollows of the cheeks, and along the frown lines. Add the black outlines and white highlights with a fine brush. Finish with a thin line of red under the eyes.*

# Introduction

**Have you ever wondered how a professional makeup artist can turn ordinary-looking actors into terrifying monsters or aliens, or make them look as though they have been injured in an accident?** This book will show you how to create some fabulous special effects using makeup and materials that are easily obtained and simple to use. If you are new to face painting, take time to look at the four step-by-step photographs of the green monster below before you try more difficult faces. These show you the basic techniques of applying water-based face paint with a sponge and brush.

▲ *A costume can make all the difference when creating a really effective character. It's a good idea to start a collection of fabric, clothing, wigs, and accessories to go with your face-painting designs.*

*Fabric shapes sewn on a black skirt.*

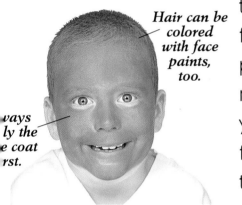

*Hair can be colored with face paints, too.*

*vays ly the e coat rst.*

**1** Cover the whole face with green paint, using a slightly damp sponge. Add a second coat if necessary to strengthen the color.

*Paint outlines of larger shapes first, then fill in with color.*

*Apply one color at a time.*

**2** Paint the red eyebrows with a large brush. Then add red markings on the cheeks and beside the eyes.

*Paint lighter colors over darker ones.*

**3** Paint sharp white fangs at the sides of the mouth, then add a flash of white at the corner of each eyebrow.

*Add dark or black outlines last.*

**4** Outline the nostrils, lips, and fangs in black. Add spiky black eyebrows and finish with black spots all over the face.

# Materials

*Glitter gels are a fun extra and great for fantasy faces.*

Today, you can buy all kinds of exciting special-effects materials and a range of bright face-painting colors. You should be able to find face paints in most toy and hobby stores. Make sure they are the kind that wash off with water. Avoid greasy stick makeup that is hard to remove from faces and clothes. If you have a lot of materials, store them in an airtight box or buy a special carrying case.

▲ *A good selection of colors, several sponges, and a range of different-sized brushes is essential.*

A BASIC FX FACE-PAINTING KIT includes a set of water-based face paints, three or four brushes and sponges, a towel to wrap around your model's neck, a container for water, some special-effects wax, a stipple sponge, a plastic spatula, crepe hair, a bald cap, and some fake blood.

*Plastic balls used to create alien heads (see page 26).*

◀ *Bald caps can be bought from special theatrical suppliers or novelty stores. Thin caps are more effective than thick ones but are more expensive.*

▲ Crepe hair is made of wool. It comes in tightly woven braids in many natural hair colors.

▶ A stipple sponge is used to texture face paint or wax. Special-effects wax can be molded into false noses or used as a light adhesive. Fake blood comes in a gel or liquid. Use it carefully—it can stain clothes.

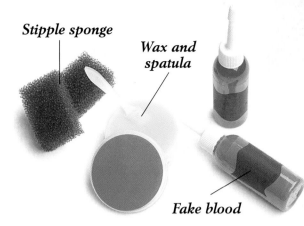

Stipple sponge

Wax and spatula

Fake blood

▼ Always keep your containers, brushes, and towels very clean and change the water regularly.

# Aging the Face

**Base coat should match model's skin color.**

**1** Apply a light brown base coat over the whole face with a dry sponge, then paint on the white highlights with a brush.

Once you know how to apply basic face paints you can start to practice the special-effects technique of aging a face. This is the first skill taught in makeup school, and it involves an understanding of bone structure, shading, and highlighting. It's not as hard as it sounds, and it will help you to make your characters much more realistic.

**Paint the ears, too.**

**2** Deepen the wrinkles and shade around the eyes and cheeks and down the sides of the nose in gray.

# Grandpa

**T**O AGE A FACE, start by studying your own reflection in a mirror. Scrunch up your face to see where wrinkle lines will appear when you get older. Feel the sunken areas around your eyes and the hollows of your cheeks. Then feel where the bones are more prominent—your forehead, nose, chin, and cheekbones. When aging a face, you need to shade the sunken areas and highlight the more prominent areas.

**Paint thin red lines in the lips.**

**Sponge white paint into the hair.**

**Whiten the eyebrows with a brush.**

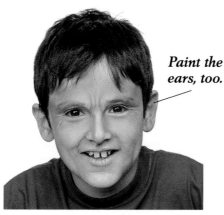

**3** Blend the areas of white and gray with a dry sponge, then dab red on the cheeks with a stipple sponge for broken veins.

**4** For a more unkempt appearance, dab a little dark brown face paint over the forehead, cheeks, and chin with a dry sponge.

▶ *Grandpa is wearing an old tweed jacket and wool scarf. You could also add eyeglass frames with the glass removed.*

8

*If necessary, darken the hair with black paint and paint a V-shaped hairline with a brush.*

# COUNT DRACULA AND HIS BRIDE

◄ *Buy or make a large black cape for Dracula. His bride is wearing a long white dress and a veil made from an old lace curtain attached to a piece of elastic.*

**D**RACULA IS THE MOST FAMOUS VAMPIRE of all time and is a popular character for parties, particularly at Halloween. Both these faces have been created using the aging techniques described on the previous page. Add a smudge of red paint under the eyes to make them appear bloodshot, and use a fine brush to paint on the feathery eyebrows. Finish by adding white fangs outlined in black. We've painted a touch of red on the tips of the fangs, or you could use a few drops of fake blood instead.

► *To paint Count Dracula's skull-like companion, apply a white base, sponge on pale yellow and purple for a textured effect, then add the black patches. (See page 2 for a larger picture to follow.)*

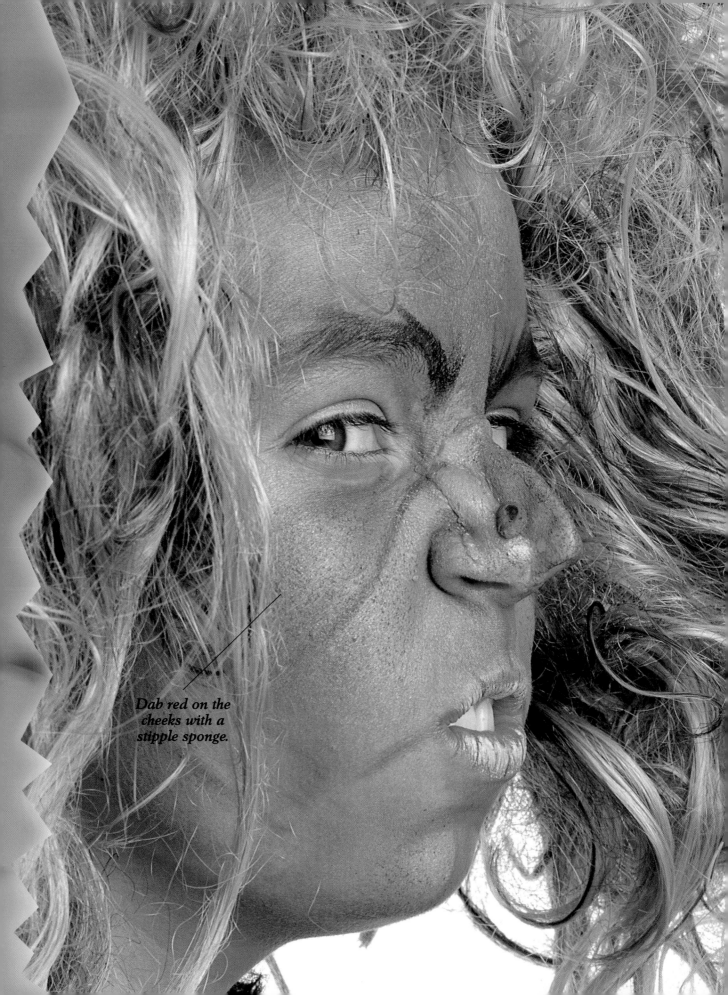

*Dab red on the
cheeks with a
stipple sponge.*

# Shaping the Face

Makeup artists use special wax or nose putty to change the shape of a nose, add pointed ears or chins, or to create bags under the eyes. Wax is a lot of fun to use and extremely versatile. It can be also be used to create scars and wounds, or even as a light adhesive. The best kind of wax to buy is one that will stick directly to clean, dry skin but will wash off easily in warm water. When you want to remove the wax, scrape most of it off with your fingers, then wash away the rest. You may need to use cold cream to remove oil-based wax.

▲ *Practice a range of different nose shapes—a hook nose as shown above, a bumpy monster nose, or a turned-up pixie nose.*

## Horrible Hag

◄ *To complete the character, we've added a wig but have put it on upside down. Find out more about wigs on page 20.*

**O**UR SCARY HAG has a hook nose, complete with wart. The wart is simply a piece of breakfast cereal, stuck to the side of the nose with a tiny piece of wax. Once you have shaped the nose, apply your face paint. Here, we've sponged on a green base coat, brushed a little red under the eyes, and added black feathery eyebrows.

**1** Soften a small piece of wax between your fingers, roll it into a ball, and position it on the center of the nose.

**2** Mold the wax into shape with your fingers or with a spatula, then smooth the edges onto the skin.

# Boily Face

**ERE, SPECIAL-EFFECTS WAX** has been applied all over the face to create an effective ghoul with nasty green boils. When applying the wax, make sure you smooth down the edges so that it will stick to the skin. Once the wax has been on the skin for a while, it will get warmer and begin to wrinkle, giving the surface more texture. You can use wax to shape the face in other ways. Try designing a new character with a thick ridge running across the eyebrows or with a wide bulbous nose.

*Press onto the skin.*

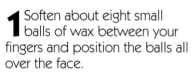

**1** Soften about eight small balls of wax between your fingers and position the balls all over the face.

*Cobweb hair bought from a novelty store.*

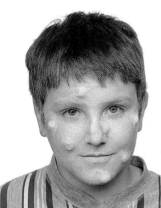

**2** Dab on a pale green base coat with a sponge or thick brush. Apply several coats to build up the color.

*Paint in aging lines with a brush.*

**3** Sponge purple paint over the wax boils and add patches of dark green around the eyes, nose, and chin.

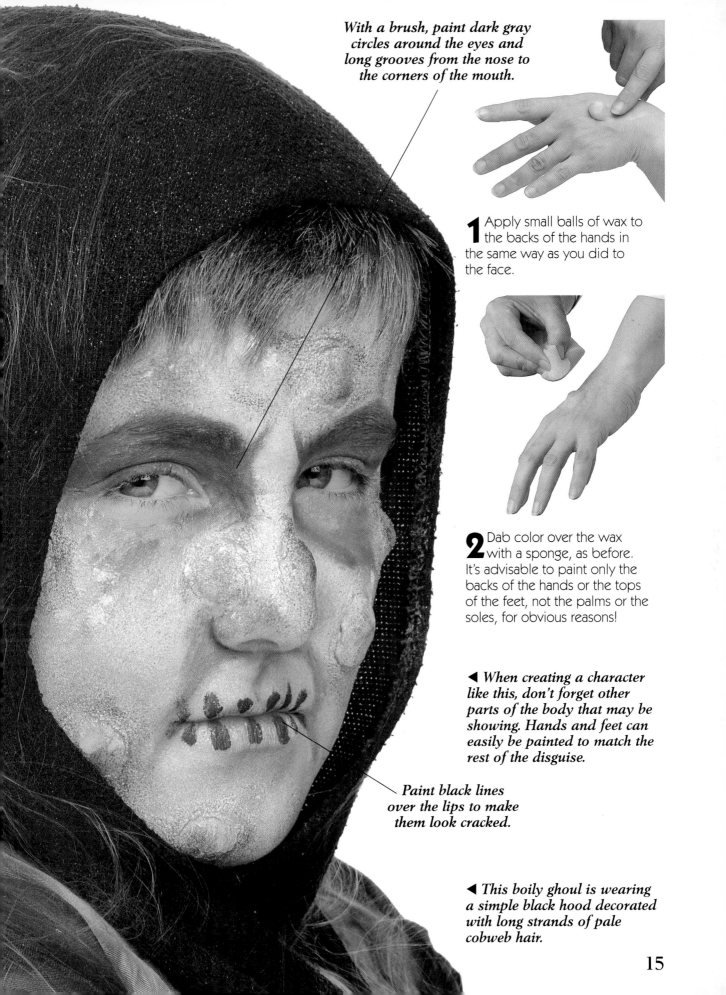

*With a brush, paint dark gray circles around the eyes and long grooves from the nose to the corners of the mouth.*

**1** Apply small balls of wax to the backs of the hands in the same way as you did to the face.

**2** Dab color over the wax with a sponge, as before. It's advisable to paint only the backs of the hands or the tops of the feet, not the palms or the soles, for obvious reasons!

◄ *When creating a character like this, don't forget other parts of the body that may be showing. Hands and feet can easily be painted to match the rest of the disguise.*

*Paint black lines over the lips to make them look cracked.*

◄ *This boily ghoul is wearing a simple black hood decorated with long strands of pale cobweb hair.*

15

# Pirates Ahoy!

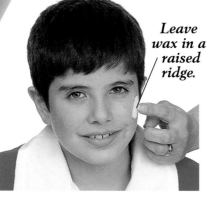

*Leave wax in a raised ridge.*

**1** Soften a small piece of wax between your fingers, mold it into a hot dog shape, and position it on the cheek.

**2** Use a plastic spatula or a similar blunt tool to make a groove running down the whole length of the wax.

*Paint on fake blood with a fine brush.*

**3** Apply red and black paint with a stipple sponge to create a bruised effect, then paint on the fake blood with a fine brush.

**I**N ACTION AND ADVENTURE MOVIES, or when making a television show about hospitals, the makeup artist often has to create realistic injuries and scars. With just a little special-effects wax and some fake blood, you can create wounds that will send your friends rushing for the first-aid kit. Be extra careful when using theatrical blood, because it may stain clothes. If you don't want to use fake blood, you can apply red face paint instead. However, it won't look quite as effective.

*Let a little fake blood dribble down the cheek.*

▶ *Once you have created the wounds, sponge a thin coat of light brown over the face. The girl pirate's face has been aged slightly using dark brown shading and the techniques described on page 8. Paint over the eyebrows in black and, for an unshaven look, dab a little black paint around the chin with a stipple sponge.*

Bandannas and bright
vests complete the
pirate disguise.

Paint a
thin black
mustache.

# Fantastic Fish

**THIS FANTASTIC FISH** has been created by sticking paper scales (here, torn out of ordinary paper towels) to the face with a thin layer of special-effects wax. The scales have then been sponged with orange water-based face paint. When applying face paint to paper, you need to make your sponge much wetter than usual because the paper absorbs a lot of water. Keep the paint thick and apply more coats if you think that the color looks thin. Use wax and torn paper to create other amazing creatures, such as a green scaly dragon.

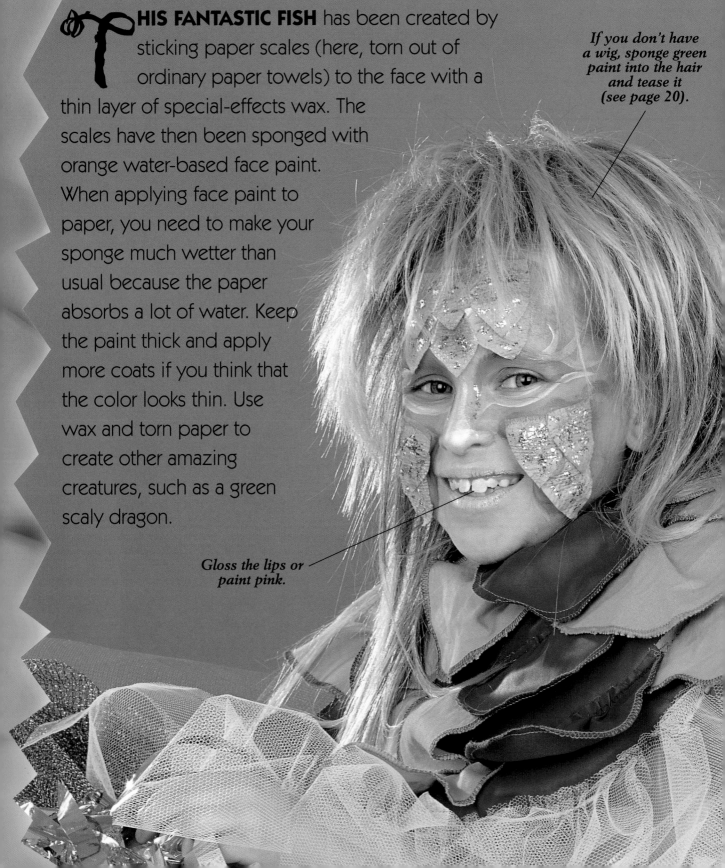

*If you don't have a wig, sponge green paint into the hair and tease it (see page 20).*

*Gloss the lips or paint pink.*

*Tie back long hair.*

*Keep the layer of wax thin.*

*Press gently until it sticks.*

*Dab on the paint so that you don't tear the paper.*

**1** Soften a small amount of special-effects wax between your fingers and smooth it over the forehead and cheekbones. Work quickly so the wax doesn't dry out.

**2** Have plenty of torn paper scales ready before you apply the wax. Lay the scales over the wax, slightly overlapping each one.

**3** Dab orange face paint over the paper scales with a sponge, taking the paint over the cheeks and forehead.

*Add a green or blue wig to complete the fishy look.*

▼ *To create this costume, long thin strips of tulle, net, and shiny fabric have been attached to a collar made out of large satin fish scales.*

**4** Paint pale blue around the eyes, then outline the scales in the same color. Add touches of silver glitter for extra sparkle.

# Changing the Hair

To make a character look really complete, you shouldn't forget to pay attention to the hair. Hair can be slicked back with hair gel, painted with water-based face paints, or sprayed with colored or glitter hair spray. It's also worth starting a collection of wigs and hairpieces (lengths of hair that are attached to the model's hair with hairpins). On the next page, you can find out how to use crepe hair to make a mustache and beard.

▲ *Metallic glitter wigs like these are available in many costume and novelty stores and are not expensive to buy. They come in a wide range of colors and are good for fantasy faces.*

▶ *Paint hair with water-based face paints using a damp sponge or large brush. The lighter the hair color, the more vibrant the color will become. Water-based face paints will wash out easily with shampoo.*

*Colored hair spray (When using hair spray, always shield the eyes.)*

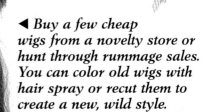

◀ *Buy a few cheap wigs from a novelty store or hunt through rummage sales. You can color old wigs with hair spray or recut them to create a new, wild style.*

▼ *A wild character needs a wild hair style. To make long hair wild and tangled, hold it in small sections and run a fine-tooth comb through it backward, pushing strands of hair toward the scalp. Here, we've tied in ribbons, strips of net, and shiny mesh to complete the effect.*

# THE WIZARD

*Color the hair with white water-based face paint to match the beard.*

**W**E'VE USED WHITE CREPE HAIR to create this wizard's long, flowing mustache and beard. Crepe hair comes in different shades of tightly curled strands that are wound into a long braid. You can attach crepe hair to clean, dry skin with wax or with a water-soluble spirit gum (a liquid adhesive used by many professional makeup artists). If you use spirit gum, test it on a small skin patch first—it may cause irritation.

◀ *Paint your wizard's face with a fantasy design. Here, we've used bright colors and bold, sweeping brush strokes.*

**1** Sponge on a base coat, then smooth a thin layer of wax right under the nose and over the chin. Pat the wax gently with your fingers to make it tacky, so the hair can easily stick to it.

*Comb through the beard, then cut it into a point once it has been fixed in position.*

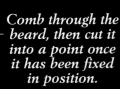

**2** Cut the hair into appropriate lengths and gently separate the coiled strands to make four or five thin layers. Mix different colors for a more natural look.

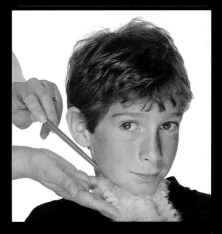

**3** Attach each layer of hair, starting from the bottom of the chin and working upward. Use the end of a brush to coax the hair into place.

# Mad Scientist

*Cut cap over ears.*

**1** Sponge yellow all over the face. If you are using a white or skin-colored bald cap, paint that, too.

**O**UR MAD SCIENTIST has turned a strange color and has lost most of his hair in his last experiment. . . . This effect looks professional but is actually very easy to do. It uses crepe hair again (here, dark brown) and a bald cap. We used a thin yellow swimming cap for this character, but you can also buy special latex or plastic caps from a theatrical supplier or novelty store. Thinner caps look better than thick ones, but they cost more and can tear. Once the bald cap is in position, trim off any excess plastic around the forehead and ears with scissors.

*Dab paint over natural eyebrows.*

**2** Using a sponge, shade the area around the eyes, the hollows of the cheeks, and the chin with brown.

*Use a little at a time.*

*Water-soluble spirit gum*

**4** Attach crepe hair to the cap layer by layer, as shown on page 23, using water-soluble spirit gum or wax. Once the crepe hair is in position, gently comb it through.

*Stick eyebrows on the cap, not the skin.*

*Attach the sideburns to the cap right in front of the ears.*

**3** Use a fine brush to outline the eyes and lips and add wrinkles. Attach crepe hair eyebrows and sideburns with spirit gum or wax.

*Sponge paint on the hands to match.*

▶ *The mad scientist is wearing an old tweed jacket and a wool scarf. Characters created with bald caps are fun, but remember that if you wear a bald cap to a party, it can get hot and uncomfortable after a while.*

# False Parts

Adding false parts to your characters can look really effective. Makeup artists create some amazing special effects for movies and television using liquid plastics that are painted directly on the skin, or by giving actors specially made false body parts. On this and the next two pages we'll show you how you can create some really simple effects at home, using a lightweight ball and some easy-to-make gelatin skin.

*▲ Here, we've painted the ball, face, and ears green, and the lips pink. We've used black to shade the head and face and outline the lips and eyes.*

# Brainy Aliens

**T**HESE ALIEN HEADS are lightweight balls with large holes cut into them so that they sit on the head. On the green alien, the ball has been cut to shape over the forehead and sits just above the eyebrows. The orange head has been cut into a point between the eyebrows. Stick some foam strips inside the ball for comfort.

*▶ Apply an orange base all over with a sponge and blend in red at the sides of the face. Paint the green and black patches around the forehead, cheeks, and chin with a wide brush, then add the bands over the eyes, following the shape of the eyebrows. Paint the white teeth over your model's mouth and outline in black.*

*▼ Our alien's tunic is just long strips of torn colored fabric attached to an elastic collar.*

# Flaky Face

**T** **O MAKE FALSE SKIN,** you just need to heat gelatin and glycerin with a little water (see the recipe below). You can buy gelatin in supermarkets and glycerin in a drugstore. Makeup artists call this "skin gel" and use it to produce all kinds of effects, including realistic-looking burns. Here, we've used it to create a face with flaking skin.

▶ *Complete the character by adding dark green shading around the eyes, nose, and mouth. Brush purple below the eyes and add a few drops of fake blood or red paint.*

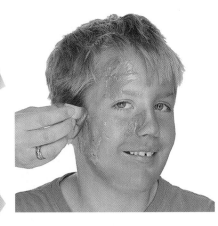

**1** Dip a piece of false skin into a cup of hot water for 30 seconds, or until it becomes slightly tacky. Position the false skin onto the face, smooth side down. It will stick immediately. Once the false skin is in position, dab on your base coat with a sponge.

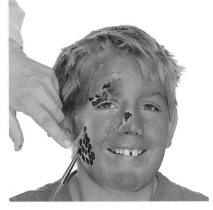

**2** Gently peel back some of the false skin and paint a design underneath. Here, we've painted a reptile skin in yellow and green.

## How to Make False Skin*

**1** *Put three heaping tablespoons of gelatin and two tablespoons of glycerin into a saucepan and add enough water to make the mixture the consistency of mashed potato.*

**2** *Gently heat the mixture until all the glycerin has dissolved into a liquid and you can pour it off a spoon.*

**3** *Cover a tray or cutting board with plastic wrap and paint the mixture onto the wrap in patches or strips, depending on what size and shape you want the false skin to be. When set, gently peel the skin from the plastic wrap.*

28

* Not recommended for children under 12 without adult supervision.

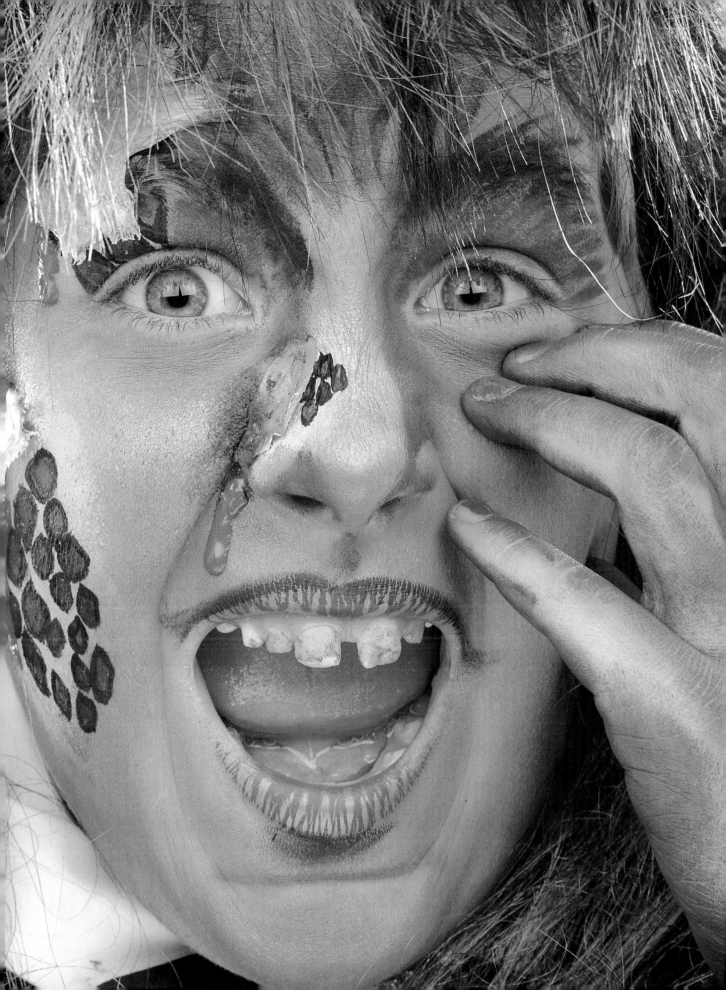

# Three-Eyed Ghoul

*Red paint or fake blood completes this ghoulish character.*

**F**ALSE EYES can be bought from a novelty store and can look horribly realistic. They are easily stuck to the face with a little special-effects wax. The false eye on this face was made using the recipe for false skin on page 28. To make a good eye shape, pour the mixture into a small wineglass and let it set for a couple of hours. Once set, scoop the eye out of the glass. Stick the flat side to the face with wax and paint the rounded side with ordinary face paints, as shown in the photographs. This can be done before or after the eye is fixed in position.

▶ *Sponge light gray over the whole face, then pink on the forehead, eyes, and cheeks. Darken the eyebrows with black and add shadows under the eyes. Outline the nostrils, then paint the mouth black and white.*

*Smooth down the edges with your fingers.*

**1** Making sure the skin is clean and dry, fix the eye in the center of the forehead with special-effects wax.

**2** Build up the edges of the false eye with wax to make a socket. This will also help keep the eye firmly in place.

# Gallery

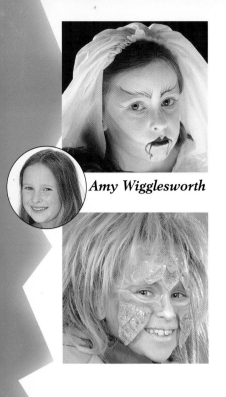

Amy Wigglesworth

**T**HE PUBLISHERS would like to thank the models—who look very different without their makeup—and face painters Lauren Staton, Wilhelmina Barnden and Jacqueline Russon.

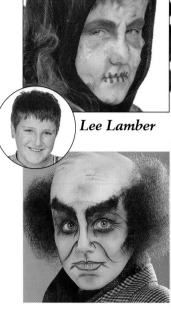

Lee Lamber

Amy Wigglesworth

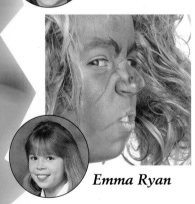

Scott Lamber

Luke Lamber

Patrick Milburn

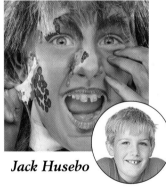

Emma Ryan

Jack Husebo

Colin Capp

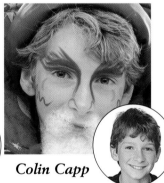

KINGFISHER
*Larousse Kingfisher Chambers Inc.*
*95 Madison Avenue New York, New York 10016*

*First edition 1997*
10 9 8 7 6 5 4 3 2 1
Copyright © In-Resort Services Ltd 1997
*All rights reserved under International and Pan-American Copyright Conventions*

LIBRARY OF CONGRESS CATALOGING-IN-PUBLICATION DATA
*FX Faces / Snazaroo.*
      *p.   cm.*
    *Summary: Shows how professional makeup artists use makeup and other tools to create fabulous and scary special effects, like a three-eyed ghoul, mad scientist, and horrible hag.*
    *ISBN 0-7534-5054-2*
    *1. Face painting—Juvenile literature. 2. Theatrical makeup—Juvenile literature.*
*[1. Face painting.]   I. Snazaroo (Firm).*
*TT911.F84  1997*
*792'.027—dc21   96-38047  CIP AC*
*Printed in Hong Kong*

Luke Freeman